Writing Complete Affective Objectives:

A Short Course

Writing Complete Affective Objectives:

A Short Course

Blaine Nelson Lee
M. David Merrill

Brigham Young University

Wadsworth Publishing Company, Inc.
Belmont, California

ISBN-0-534-00185-8
L. C. Cat. Card No.: 72-87732

Printed in the United States
of America

1 2 3 4 5 6 7 8 9 10 —

76 75 74 73 72

To keep the price of this book as low
as possible, we have utilized an economical
means of typesetting. We welcome your
comments.

This book is for people who are concerned about attitudes--measuring them, observing them, developing them, and changing them. If you know something about behavior objectives in general and are now anxious to affect the attitudes of learners, you are ready for this book. We assume that you are not only concerned about what people *can* do but that you are also concerned about what they *will* do. This is the focus of an affective objective.

This book is self-instructional. As you proceed you will be given directions to follow, information to consider, and choices to make. In approximately one hour (average completion time is sixty-five minutes) you will be able to write complete affective objectives for any subject at any age level--for a child, a student, an employer, or a friend. Most of the examples are from elementary and secondary education, but the process of writing affective objectives is the same for any topic that has attitudes associated with it.

This book was developed and tested after the pattern established by the Department of Instructional Research and Development at Brigham Young University. The book was pilot tested with three groups: a group of naive college sophomores, a group of preservice teachers, and a group of professors of education. After some modification the book was subjected to a control group validation study with secondary preservice teachers at Brigham Young University. (The average gain from pretest to posttest was significant $p < .001$). The book was then field tested with in-service elementary and secondary teachers in a Title III project, Widefield School District, Colorado. Participants who have successfully used this book range in experience from preservice teachers to teachers with over fifty years of experience.

The creative approaches *you* use to influence students will determine your success in developing positive student attitudes; affective objectives will help you to measure that success.

Because this is primarily a program for teachers, the approach is not based on the use of any of the many standard psychological measures that are available for assessing personality variables. The aim is to help teachers discover enough about student attitudes so that some decisions can be made--decisions about the kind of teaching that could more successfully influence learners. (That such influence *ought* to take place in schools is not the argument here. The ethical implications of behavioral and attitudinal manipulation are discussed elsewhere and are beyond the scope of this book. We merely assume that students are influenced, for better or for worse, by those who teach them.) This program will provide help for the teacher who wants to assess in some way the influence he has on his students.

We are dealing with attitudes and feelings, as these find expression in behavior, but it is behavior that we must ultimately deal with. If there appear to be inconsistencies between a person's supposed attitudes and his acts, to which do we give credence? We view with skepticism a person who avows support for something *yet does nothing* to support it. Parents often find to their chagrin that children have modeled their behavior rather than their preachments. A professor who lectured each semester on the virtues of audiovisual aids was continually surprised that his students did not become motivated to use audiovisual aids. The students were learning, but from what he *did*, not from what he *said*.

Each day in countless little ways we decide in a similar manner what people feel by what we observe them do.

In summary:

1. This program is designed to help teachers analyze student behaviors that may indicate attitudes and feelings.

2. We focus on behavior because that approach is useful and productive for us.

Note:

If this book is to be used as a text, a set of instructor and learner materials is available. * Materials include:

a. Summary of validation procedures
b. Instructor's manual
c. Terminal and enabling objectives
d. Diagnostic pretest and posttest
e. Instructor's key and diagnostic prescription

---

*Available from: Department of Instructional Research and Development, Brigham Young University, Provo, Utah 84601.

PROGRAM OBJECTIVE

Given a written description of a learning situation and an attitude to be demonstrated, you will be able to write an original, complete affective objective.

1. A high-probability student approach behavior that is observable by the teacher will be described.

2. Realistic criteria that can be used to assess a pattern of approach will be specified.

3. A free-choice, no-cue situation in which the approach behavior may occur will be described.

4. The attitude to be demonstrated will be described.

1. People do things.

2. The things people do can be observed.

3. The things people do follow patterns.

4. We learn about people as we observe them.

5. We make judgments about people based on what we observe.

6. Our judgments are useful if they allow us to predict with some accuracy what people will do.

7. By comparing our predictions with what we observe people do, we can increase the accuracy of our predictions.

These seven statements are a simplified expression of the conceptual orientation with which this program was written. There are other ways to view behavior; this approach provides a logical method for analyzing the behavior of learners, and it has proven useful to us. Introspection and some personal analysis have suggested that people make judgments about other people. This program describes a way to gather information more systematically and to make judgments more objectively and thus more reliably than we otherwise would.

CONTENTS

Why Look at Affective Objectives Our Way?

DEDICATION

To the I-STEP staff, who showed that educators can make a difference . . .

To the I-STEP students, who helped pilot the original pro-gram . . .

To Dr. Hugh Baird, who started the process . . .

To Shawny, who is understanding . . .

To Blaine Christian, who will understand some day . . .

1

What is
an Affective Objective?

Measuring and Changing Student Attitudes

The word *affect*, when used in the educational sense, refers to attitudes, feelings, emotions, interests, or appreciations. A behavioral objective that deals with affect focuses on the attitudes, feelings, emotions, interests, or appreciations of students.

GO TO THE NEXT PAGE

Listed below are parts of complete objectives. Check the statements which are probably parts of *affective* objectives.

___a. Students will show their interest in learning rhythms by . . .

___b. At least one-half the students will solve all geometry problems correctly . . .

___c. By voluntarily visiting one of the national parks, the student will demonstrate his concern for . . .

___d. All students will demonstrate the forward roll . . .

TURN THE PAGE

If you checked *b* and/or *d* TURN TO PAGE 7.

If you checked *a* and/or *c* TURN TO PAGE 6.

Which of the following deal with attitudes, feelings, or emotions?

___a. Appreciation for French culture

___b. Dislike of swimming

___c. Interest in finger painting

___d. Concern for reptiles

TURN TO PAGE 9

Both *a* and *c* are parts of complete affective objectives.

a. Students will show their interest in learning rhythms by . . .

c. By voluntarily visiting one of the national parks, the student will demonstrate his concern for . . .

In *a*, the phrase that indicates attitude is "show their interest."

In *c*, the phrase that indicates attitude is "demonstrate his concern for."

TURN TO PAGE 8

You said that one or both of these could be parts of affective objectives:

b. At least one-half the students will solve all geometry problems without . . .

d. All students will demonstrate the forward roll . . .

Admittedly, the way a person performed these two tasks might reflect an attitude, but are any attitudes or interests specifically mentioned?

These two statements are *not* parts of affective objectives.

Remember: *affective objectives deal with attitudes, emotions, interests, or appreciations.*

TURN BACK TO PAGE 5

Affective objectives deal with students' attitudes, but the word *attitude* is somewhat vague.

Can you see or hear or taste or measure an attitude?

Can you observe attitudes?

No, attitudes cannot be directly observed. Yet, think of someone who likes you. How do you know they like you? Have you measured their affection?

If you think attitudes can be measured directly, TURN TO PAGE 11.

If you think attitudes cannot be measured directly, TURN TO PAGE 10.

ALL of the statements refer to attitudes.

Remember: *affective objectives deal with attitudes.*

GO BACK TO PAGE 8

Attitudes cannot be measured directly.

How then do we measure attitudes?

You were asked to analyze how you knew that someone liked you. If you thought about it, your response may have been something like this:

——He opens the door for me.

——She smiles when she sees me.

——He sent me a card on my birthday.

——She asked my opinion.

——She looks at me when I'm talking.

——He goes places with me.

TURN TO PAGE 12

You said that you think attitudes can be measured directly.

Perhaps someday we will be able to measure a person's attitudes like we measure weight or length or volume, but at present that is not possible. Behavioral scientists are able to measure a galvanic skin response (used in lie-detector tests), pulse, rate of breathing, etc., and these are indicators of how a person is "feeling." But even so, these are *indirect measures*. We can only infer hate or love or anger from the pattern of responses recorded.

Attitudes cannot be measured directly.

GO BACK TO PAGE 10

Those thoughts may not be exactly what you were thinking, but they probably represent the kind of thing you were thinking about.

Perhaps you noticed that each of the statements listed indi-cated a *behavior* :

goes places	opens the door
sent a card	asked my opinion
smiles	looks at me

How do we determine attitude?

GO TO THE NEXT PAGE

Remember: we infer attitudes from what we observe people
say and do.

2

The Behavior
in an Affective Objective
What Do Students Do?

Suppose you observed a friend, Mike, doing the following:

1. On three occasions he shopped at a hobby shop.

2. He purchased four model airplanes.

3. He spent three hours each afternoon building the models.

4. He went to the city park on Saturday to fly his planes.

What attitude would Mike be demonstrating?

a. Dislike for girls

b. Interest in model railroads

c. Concern for old records

d. Love for model airplanes

GO TO THE NEXT PAGE

That was fairly obvious, wasn't it? Mike likes model air-planes.

The reason you could choose correctly, even though you do not know Mike, is that all the behaviors described were ones that showed Mike doing something with model airplanes. In this case, every activity you observed brought Mike into close contact with model airplanes.

When someone's activity tends to bring him into contact with (tends to cause him to approach) a particular subject, we call that activity an *approach behavior*.

From the approach behaviors we observed it was easy to decide what Mike's attitude toward model airplanes was.

TURN THE PAGE

Besides showing attitudes by the subjects we approach, we also indicate attitudes by what we do not approach.

Suppose Mike's friend, Bill, was with him in each of the situations already mentioned, and you observed the following:

1. Bill waited outside the hobby store while Mike shopped.

2. Bill never bought any model airplanes.

3. Bill spent each afternoon fishing.

4. While Mike was flying his planes Bill would watch the girls in the park.

How would you describe Bill's attitude toward model airplanes?

a. Enthusiastic about model airplanes

b. Mildly interested in model airplanes

c. No interest in model airplanes

GO TO THE NEXT PAGE

Bill shows no interest in model airplanes; *c* is the correct answer.

Bill's behavior with model airplanes is very different from Mike's. Mike approached the subject, but Bill did not.

Bill's attitude is *neutral*.

A third friend, Sam, has been observed doing the following:

1. When Bill and Mike went to the park to fly airplanes, Sam refused to go.

2. Sam gave away a model airplane kit that he had received for Christmas.

3. Sam will not go to the hobby shop with Mike.

4. Sam never visited Mike while Mike was building his models.

How would you describe Sam's attitude toward model air-planes?

TURN THE PAGE

Sam avoided the subject of model airplanes. Sam's activities, those that took him away from the subject, are called *avoidance behaviors*.

The examples of behavior given so far have been relatively easy to classify as approach, neutral, or avoidance behaviors. Many behaviors are more difficult to classify. For example, if a person bought a model airplane but never built it, would that be an approach behavior or an avoidance behavior?

GO TO THE NEXT PAGE

It could be either one, depending on what *else* the person did about the subject of model airplanes. You can see that the more you know about a person's total behavior, the better you are able to judge his tendency to approach or avoid specific subjects.

TURN THE PAGE

All three kinds of behavior--approach, neutral, and avoid-ance--can be indicators of student attitude.

However, because the focus of this book is primarily on student attitudes toward topics taught in school and because the desired student attitude is shown by *approach,* approach behaviors will be used in the objectives in this book.

Some topics, such as smoking or the use of drugs, may have avoidance behaviors as the desired outcome. For a dis-cussion of the use of avoidance behaviors in affective objec-tives, see the Appendix.

A complete affective objective includes specific student ap-proach behaviors.

GO TO THE NEXT PAGE

So an affective objective is based on an approach behavior.

But there is a great variety of possible approach behaviors for any given attitude. How do you choose an appropriate behavior to observe?*

Suppose you want to assess student attitude toward English. One student behavior that would indicate approach to the subject would be stealing hubcaps every night for a month to get enough money to attend a Shakespeare festival in New York. Granted that this could be considered an approach behavior, is it one that you could expect of many students?

_____a. Yes

_____b. No

TURN THE PAGE

---

*A detailed listing and classification of behaviors that indicate attitude may be found in David Krathwohl, Benjamin S. Bloom, and Bertram B. Massia, *Taxonomy of Educational Objectives, Handbook II: Affective Domain* (New York: David McKay Company, Inc. 1964).

No. Few students would exhibit this behavior, and even if they did, you might not be pleased with their means of obtaining the money.

To be useful in an affective objective, an approach behavior must be likely to occur commonly among students who like the subject. Because there is a strong likelihood that this type of behavior will occur, we call this *high-probability* behavior.

The behavior that you specify in an affective objective should be high-probability approach behavior.

GO TO THE NEXT PAGE

How do you know what kinds of behavior are high-probability approach behaviors? The easiest way is to observe someone who has a known interest in the subject. What things does he commonly do to approach the subject? You have been given an example of a student who likes model airplanes; his approach behaviors (buying, building, flying the planes) were fairly common ones. The more *you* know about a topic, the easier it will be for you to specify common, high-probability approach behaviors.

If you are teaching a course for the first time or are not familiar with anyone who knows the subject matter, you may have difficulty determining high-probability behaviors initially. General behaviors may need to be used, such as *taking the time to encounter the subject* or *going to sources of information about the subject*. Ultimately you will determine high-probability behaviors by what you observe people do.

TURN THE PAGE

Note:

Low-probability behaviors may occur and will certainly indicate approach or avoidance, but you cannot count on them to occur. You should plan for behaviors that you are relatively sure will occur.

GO TO THE NEXT PAGE

As we have seen, the behavior we are concerned with in af-fective objectives has the following characteristics:

a. It is observable.

b. It is a high-probability behavior.

c. It indicates approach.

Statements *b* and *c* have been discussed in some detail. Let us turn our attention briefly to what is meant by "observable."

Before you can make a judgment about a student's behavior, you must have some evidence of the behavior. If a sixth-grade student stayed awake reading about South America every night until 3 A.M. but no one knew about it, would you have any evidence that he liked geography?

_____a. Yes

_____b. No

TURN THE PAGE

You would *not* have any evidence that he liked geography.

(You would probably be able to tell that he had been getting little sleep, but unless he told you what he had been doing, you could only guess.)

We can only make judgments about what we observe.

There are two ways we can observe behavior--directly and indirectly.

Direct observation: Student activity that you actually see

Indirect observation: Student activity that is reported to you

GO TO THE NEXT PAGE

Which of the following would be direct observations? Indirect observations?

You are a high school math teacher

___ a. Students explain their feelings about math in an anonymous questionnaire.

___ b. In the bookstore downtown you meet a student purchasing a paperback math book.

___ c. The English teacher tells you that one of your students has volunteered to give an oral report on modern math.

___ d. Five students fall asleep during your class presentation.

TURN THE PAGE

In situations *b* and *d* you actually see the student's activity. These are direct observations. In **situation** *a* the students report their feelings. In situation *d* another teacher reports the activity.

Situations *a* and *c* are examples of *indirect* observation.

If you chose incorrectly, you may wish to review the definitions given on page 27 before continuing.

Remember: *Indirect:* *the behavior is reported to you.*

Direct: *you personally observe the behavior.*

Both direct and indirect observations are useful in assessing attitudes.

GO TO THE NEXT PAGE

SUMMARY

The *behavior* you include in an affective objective should:

1. Be directly or indirectly observable.

2. Be high-probability behavior.

3. Indicate approach.

Indicate which of the following are appropriate statements of behavior for an affective objective.

Attitude: enthusiasm for oil painting

___a. Student goes two days without eating to finish a painting.

___b. Student thinks about Leonardo da Vinci all day.

___c. Student enters oil painting in local contest; contest entries reported in newspaper.

___d. Student completes an oil painting in class but throws it away before the teacher sees it.

___e. Student pulls the bristles out of his paint brushes.

___f. Student tears pages out of art books in the library.

___g. Teacher overhears a student telling his friend that he has visited two art museums.

TURN THE PAGE

___ h. Student reads comic books during art while the teacher is not looking.

___ i. Teacher receives request for recommendation from local college for a student who has applied for an art scholarship.

___ j. Student **carves** on desk during class.

GO TO THE NEXT PAGE

If you chose *c* , *g* , and *i*, you are correct. GO TO THE NEXT PAGE.

Statements *c* , *g* , and *i* contain all three elements of a behavior statement and are appropriate. If you did not choose *c*, *g*, and *i*, read below:

In statement *a* the behavior is not high-probability.

In statement *b* the behavior is not high-probability, nor is it observable.

In statement *d* the behavior is not observable.

In statement *e* the behavior is not high-probability, nor is it an approach behavior.

Statement *f* has none of the characteristics of an appropriate behavior statement.

The behavior in statement *h* is not observable, nor is it an approach behavior.

The behavior in statement *j* is not an approach behavior.

TURN THE PAGE

This concludes the section on *behavior* in an affective ob-jective. Let's see how well you have learned.

In the spaces below write *two* behaviors that could indicate "appreciation for descriptive prose." *Remember:* each be-havior must have the three characteristics listed on page 27.

1. _____

_____

2. _____

_____

GO TO THE NEXT PAGE

SELF-CHECK

Now let's check your two descriptions to see if they could qualify as statements of *behavior* in an affective objective.

a. Is a student activity described?

b. Is the activity directly observable by the teacher or indirectly observable through someone else?

c. Does the activity indicate that the students want to be associated with oil painting? (Approach)

d. Is it likely that someone who really liked oil painting would do what you have described? (High-probability)

If your answer to each of these questions is yes, then you have stated the behavior correctly. TURN THE PAGE.

If any of the questions were answered no, modify your statement on page 34. (If you are completing this program as part of a class, you may wish to talk with the instructor before continuing.)

TURN THE PAGE

3

The Conditions
in an Affective Objective

When to Evaluate Attitudes

The statement of *conditions* indicates the testing situation in which the behavior in an objective is to take place. A statement of conditions normally includes (1) an identification of what the student will have available to him (such as paper, pencil, one-half hour, a list of multiple-choice questions) and (2) what restrictions are to be placed on the student (without reference to notes, no books may be used, students must work alone, etc.).

In an affective objective the emphasis in the statement of conditions is a little different.

First, a set of alternatives must be presented to the student.

GO TO THE NEXT PAGE

There are at least two alternatives you can use:

Situation 1:

"Each student may complete his seat work or go to recess early."

Situation 2:

"Each student may complete his seat work."

Which situation allows students to choose between two *approach* responses?

TURN THE PAGE

Situation 1 allowed students to choose between two approach responses.

Situation 2 gave students a choice between responding or not responding, between completing or not completing seat work. Here the students may approach the subject or remain neutral.

Both kinds of alternatives are useful in affective objectives.

Question:

How would you likely use a situation 1 type alternative (approach versus approach)?

___ a. To determine student preferences

___ b. To rank student interests

___ c. To determine what students are not interested in

___ d. To discover dislikes of students

GO TO THE NEXT PAGE

You should have selected *a* and *b*.

If you wanted to determine student preferences between two subjects or if you wanted to rank students' interests in two or more subjects, an approach versus approach alternative might work best.

When you use the other alternative (approach versus no response) make certain that the students really feel free to refuse or not to respond to what is offered.

For example, in this situation, do you think students would feel free to refuse or not to respond?

Situation:

French teacher to class: "Unless you want your grade lowered you will all attend the French Club meeting today. Now, raise your hand if you will be at the French Club meeting. . ."

TURN THE PAGE

Few students would be willing to risk their grade by missing this meeting, and so most hands would probably be raised. In this situation the student does not really have an alternative. (By not responding he would be judged by the teacher as if he were avoiding the subject.)

GO TO THE NEXT PAGE

What the French teacher did in the last situation violated another characteristic of appropriate *conditions* in an affective objective.

The teacher must do as little as possible in the testing situation to influence which alternative a student chooses.

A situation in which a teacher does *not* influence student choice is called a *free-choice* situation.

The French teacher attempted to coerce students to attend the club meeting by basing students' grades on attendance. Other kinds of influence that teachers often give include:

extra credit	verbal approval
special favor	accepting nod or smile
privileges	pat on the back

Although these ways of influencing students may be effective in the learning situation, *none* of these is appropriate in the *testing situation*.

TURN THE PAGE

Suppose a teacher gave students a choice between volunteering or not volunteering to clean up the woodshop room. Which of the following teacher behaviors would probably not influence the student's response?

___a. Teacher makes a point of recording names of students who volunteer.

___b. Teacher has student leader ask for volunteers while teacher is out of the room.

___c. Teacher mentions that those who clean up may leave class early.

___d. Teacher asks that the shop be cleaned up, and does not observe which students do the work.

If you selected *b* and *d* , TURN TO PAGE 47.

If you selected *a* or *c* , TURN TO PAGE 46.

Two characteristics of *conditions* have now been presented: (1) at least two alternatives must be given to the student, and (2) direct teacher influence should be removed from the testing situation. The third characteristic is related to the way the student approach behavior is observed.

If the school principal walked into your class, and you asked your students to raise their hands if they liked the principal, do you think that the response would be a valid (honest) one?

        ___ a. Yes

        ___ b. No

TURN TO PAGE 47

You are incorrect.

In situations *a* and *c* the teacher has purposely done something to get students to volunteer. In situation *a* the teacher recorded the names of those who volunteered; students may assume this will make a good impression on the teacher. In situation *c* the teacher promises to reward those who volunteer by allowing them to leave class early.

In both situations the students may be volunteering not because they desire to keep the shop clean but for the more obvious reason. This kind of direct teacher influence has been removed from situations *b* and *d*.

GO TO THE NEXT PAGE

In statements *b* and *d* the teacher does not influence the student's response.

Note:

A teacher's influence cannot be removed from a *learning situation*. Even if the teacher's influence could be removed it would not be desirable, because most teachers *want* to influence their students. The kind of influence that should be eliminated when assessing attitudes in a *testing situation* is the influence that causes a student to approach a subject because of the teacher rather than because of an interest in the subject.

TURN BACK TO PAGE 45

Unless the class and the principal were both exceptional, the response would probably not be honest.

If students think they are being evaluated, they tend to respond the way they feel teachers expect them to respond.

That is, the presence of an authority figure often alters the student's response.

Therefore:

In direct observation, if you want to observe approach responses directly you must behave so that students do not feel their statements will affect their grade or your attitude toward them.

In indirect observation, if you are observing approach responses indirectly, students should not be informed that their attitudes are being evaluated.

GO TO THE NEXT PAGE

Which of these are examples of *indirect* observation?

1.   After a unit in English on descriptive adjectives, the English teacher asks the history teacher to record how often students use descriptive adjectives when they write papers for history.

2.   A health teacher asks the librarian to record the number of students who check out articles on smoking and cancer during the semester.

3.   A fifth-grade music instructor asks teachers to survey their students during regular class time to see how many would like to spend an extra hour each week singing.

4.   A second-grade teacher takes a group of students to work on art projects with another class. The paraprofessional in the other classes observes the students' work habits and reports, confidentially, to their teacher.

TURN THE PAGE

All four are examples of effective indirect observation.

The last important characteristic of the *conditions* statement in an affective objective is that the situation must be a *no-cue* situation--that is, the situation should not contain cues that indicate expected behavior. Such cues in a learning situation normally come from the teacher.

Question:

If a teacher were to tell his students as they entered a pioneer museum, "Remember our discussion about showing respect for ancestors? Do not talk or touch anything as we walk through the museum," would the teacher be providing cues that indicate expected behavior?

GO TO THE NEXT PAGE

Yes, the teacher has given the students a verbal reminder of how they are supposed to behave.

If the teacher in this situation wanted to find out if his students would show respect for the pioneers, he should say nothing to remind the students in this "testing situation." In fact, he might even have a different teacher take his students to the museum. Then he would be totally removed from the situation.

Cues that prompt the desired behavior come from what a teacher does as much as from what he says. A teacher who walks around the room with his finger to his lips during reading time is certainly communicating desirable behavior to his students. Giving verbal or nonverbal reminders of appropriate approach behaviors should not take place in the testing situation.

TURN THE PAGE

SUMMARY

In an affective objective a statement of *conditions* should:

1. Describe a *testing situation* in which the approach behavior may occur and can be observed.

2. Present at least *two alternatives* to the student.

3. Describe a *free-choice* situation, in which the teacher does not directly influence a student's choice.

4. Not indicate that attitude is being evaluated if *indirect* observations will be made.

5. Describe a situation in which students feel free to express their true feelings if *direct* observations will be made.

6. Be a *no-cue* situation in which cues that indicate expected behavior are eliminated.

GO TO THE NEXT PAGE

Explanatory note:

The statement of *conditions* is the most complex part of an affective objective. There is a good reason for this. It is usually not too difficult to determine if a specific action is approaching or avoiding a particular subject. The *interpretation* of that behavior, however, is dependent upon the conditions in which it took place. Only as you analyze the possible influencing factors (and, to the extent that you can, limit those factors to ones you have some control over) can you begin to infer an attitude.

The more control you have over the conditions in which behavior takes place, the more sure you can be of your inference.

TURN THE PAGE

Let's see how well you have learned.

Indicate which of the following are appropriate statements of conditions for observing the approach behavior "attendance at math club."

You may refer to the list of characteristics on page 52.

___ a. Math club is held weekly after school. The meetings are open to all students. The math teacher plays tennis every day after school, but periodically she reads the minutes of the club meetings, in which the names of those who attended the meeting are recorded.

___ b. Math club is held secretly once each month and is never mentioned in class.

___ c. A notice on the student bulletin board invites students to visit math club. Visitors' names are not recorded.

___ d. At the end of the semester the teacher distributes a list of math-related activities, including attendance at math club, and has students anonymously check which ones they have done.

___ e. A teacher gives a personal invitation in each math class to attend math club and states, "Your math grades will probably improve if you attend."

___ f. Teacher visits math club one afternoon and makes a mental note of which students are there.

___ g. The math teacher contacts a visiting math professor who will be speaking at the math club meeting and asks him to get a list of the students who come to hear him.

___ h. At the same time math club is held the math teacher offers help sessions to students who voluntarily desire it.

TURN TO PAGE 56

This concludes the section on *conditions* in affective objectives. Now you try writing a statement of conditions.

Situation:

A seventh-grade teacher has begun instruction on the ukulele.
A common approach behavior for students who like the ukulele
is staying after school to practice.

In the space below write appropriate conditions for observing this approach behavior.

_____

_____

_____

_____

TURN TO PAGE 57

Statements *a, d, f,* and *g* are all appropriate statements of conditions. If you marked only these, GO BACK TO PAGE 55.

If you did not select any one of these -- *a, d, f,* or *g* --look at them again. Statements *a, d,* and *g* involve indirect observation, and *f* uses direct observation. All four statements are complete.

Statement *b* lacks a testing situation and provides no alternatives to the student, because no one knows about the club meeting.

Statement *c* provides no observation, direct or indirect.

In statement *e* the teacher indicates what students ought to do (cues are provided), attempts to persuade students to attend, and thereby destroys the free-choice situation.

Statement *h* lacks most of the characteristics because it does not focus on math club attendance.

GO BACK TO PAGE 55

Use the following check list to evaluate your statement of conditions:

a. Is a testing situation described in which the approach behavior may occur? If not, TURN TO PAGE 61.

b. Are two alternatives presented to the student? If not, TURN TO PAGE 62.

c. Does the teacher do anything to directly influence the student to attend math club? If so, TURN TO PAGE 58.

d. If indirect observations are made (someone other than the teacher observes the behavior), are there any indications that attitude is being evaluated? If so, TURN TO PAGE 64.

e. If direct observations are made (the teacher personally observes the behavior) will the students feel free to express their true feelings? If not, TURN TO PAGE 60.

f. If a no-cue situation is described (in which cues that indicate expected performance have been eliminated), then TURN TO PAGE 59. If not,

TURN TO PAGE 63

Evidently you are not sure how to handle teacher influence when describing conditions. Remember that you want to assess how the student reacts to the subject matter, not how he reacts to the teacher. If the teacher rewards or punishes the student for his choice in the testing situation, the choice probably will not reflect the student's real attitude.

How could you eliminate teacher influence in the math situation?

Rewrite your statement of conditions on page 55 so that the teacher is not directly affecting what the student chooses. Then,

TURN BACK TO PAGE 57, question d

Congratulations. You have done well. You are now able to specify the most critical part of an affective objective -- the statement of conditions.

TURN TO PAGE 65

If the teacher is personally evaluating in this situation it will be readily apparent to the students. It is therefore crucial that the students realize that how they respond will not affect them or their grade. The students need to trust the teacher.

Modify your statement on page 55 so that you are making an indirect observation or so that the students really feel free to express themselves. Then,

TURN BACK TO PAGE 57, question f

If the approach behavior cannot occur, what indication will you have of any attitude? An approach behavior should always be included in an affective objective.

Rewrite your statement on page 55 to include an opportunity for an approach behavior. Then,

TURN BACK TO PAGE 57, question b

Perhaps you misunderstood the question. If the students have at least one choice, they have at least two alternatives -- to accept or reject the choice. If there are not two alternatives in the situation you described then the students must not have any choices to make.

Rewrite your statement on page 55 to provide a choice for students. Then,

TURN BACK TO PAGE 57, question c

If cues are provided that inform or remind students how they are supposed to respond, you have no way of knowing how the students would have acted on their own.

Modify your statement on page 55 to remove teacher cues that inform students of expected behavior. Then,

TURN BACK TO PAGE 59

If students realize that their attitudes are being evaluated they may not respond honestly. Someone observing for the teacher must be careful not to inform the students that their attitudes are being assessed.

Rewrite your statement on page 55 so that the students do not realize that their attitudes are being evaluated. Then,

TURN BACK TO PAGE 57, question e

If you would like to take a break, now is a good time.

When you are ready to proceed,

TURN TO PAGE 67

4

The Criteria
in an Affective Objective

How Much Change Do You Want?

We have discussed the *behavior* and *conditions* that are in-cluded in an affective objective. The third part of an affective objective is concerned with the *criteria* you use to evaluate patterns of approach and avoidance.

Whereas a statement of *conditions* describes the circum-stances in which the behavior will take place, the statement of *criteria* indicates how well or how often or how much of the approach behavior must be accomplished for the objective to be minimally achieved.

The part of an objective that specifies how you will judge com-pletion of the objective is called the statement of *criteria*.

GO TO THE NEXT PAGE

In affective objectives there are at least two kinds of criterion statements you can use; both can be affective. One kind of criterion statement:

"At least one-half the students will attend the concert . . ."

Another kind of criterion statement:

"Each student will attend at least three of the following: concert, piano recital, opera, rock festival . . . "

The first kind of criterion statement indicates the number of _____ who will demonstrate the behavior.

The second kind of criterion statement indicates the number of _____ each student will participate in.

TURN THE PAGE

The first criterion statement indicates **the** *number of students you are concerned with.*

The second criterion statement indicates the number of behaviors or activities you are concerned with.

The statement of criteria indicates how much of the behavior you would like to occur, whether this is in terms of a number of students or a number of activities.

If you think you will probably use "number of students" as a criterion, TURN TO PAGE 72.

If you think you will probably use "number of activities" as a criterion, TURN TO PAGE 75.

GUIDELINES FOR CHOOSING CRITERIA

1. First, make a judgment of how students would respond *right now* to your testing situation. (Ideally you would place the students in the testing situation and record their approach behaviors.) This is a sort of preassessment; it gives you something to compare later performance with.

2. In view of what you know about the students, choose a number that is realistic. If many students are antagonistic or disinterested in what you teach, do not expect a miracle. (If students leave your class at least as interested in the subject as they were when they entered, that is an accomplishment.)

3. The criterion you specify should be such that if the objective is accomplished, you will be able to make some generalization about the students' attitudes. (Example: "There are more students interested in math this year than there were last year.")

4. For a statement of criteria to be useful it must be specific enough so that different people will agree on what it means. Words like *some, often,* and *most* are not specific enough and do not qualify as appropriate criterion statements.

TURN TO PAGE 73

You think you will use "number of students" as a criterion for evaluating approach responses.

Whether you want 60 percent or 50 percent or 80 percent or two-thirds of your students to demonstrate the approach behavior you have chosen to observe is really up to you. In this sense a statement of criteria is very subjective. But there are guidelines which can help you choose reasonable criteria.

TURN BACK TO PAGE 71

The criterion you specify is up to you. The important thing is that you establish the criterion in such a way that if the objective is accomplished, you know something about your students' attitudes. What you should know is the proportion of your students who have favorable attitudes toward the subject you teach.

Which of the following could be appropriate criterion statements?

___ a. 56.9 percent of the students in a class of 10.

___ b. None of the students have been staying after school to work on special projects. You decide that you would like at least 85 percent of the students to stay after school.

___ c. Most of the students.

___ d. Two students in each group.

TURN THE PAGE

Statement *a* indicates a percentage that is impossible to tab-ulate for the size group suggested and is *not appropriate*.

Statement *b* expects too great a change, is unrealistic, and is *not appropriate*.

Statement *c* uses the indefinite word *most* and is *not appro-priate*.

Statement *d* has none of the problems mentioned above and is *appropriate*.

If you wish to review using "number of activities" as a cri-terion, GO TO THE NEXT PAGE.

If you have already reviewed this topic, TURN TO PAGE 80.

One of the *advantages* of using *number of activities* as a criterion is that it allows the students a greater opportunity to perform the approach behaviors. With only one approach behavior, even a high-probability behavior, there are some students who may not respond the way you hope they will *because of extenuating circumstances*. Using a number of activities lessens the possibility of this occurring.

Example:

Suppose you are assessing interest in rhyming words. The approach behavior you are observing is a voluntary listing of words that rhyme found in a daily newspaper. One of your students who normally would gladly make the list is in a class play and practices each evening, so he is unable to do the project. If you based your estimate of his interest in rhyming words on whether or not he completed the voluntary project, would your estimate be valid?

      ___a. Yes

      ___b. No

TURN THE PAGE

No. Other, outside influences prevented this student from demonstrating the approach behavior. Because this could happen for any particular approach behavior, regardless of the conditions you specify, it is an advantage to describe a number of different behaviors. Chances are that outside influences will not prevent a student from demonstrating all the approach behaviors. If more than one approach behavior is demonstrated you have more evidence from which to infer the attitude.

Of course, if you include different approach behaviors in your objective, appropriate conditions should be described for each of them.

GO TO THE NEXT PAGE

Which of the following would be appropriate criterion state-ments for assessing a number of activities?

___ a. "Several approach behaviors will be exhibited . . . "

___ b. "The student will memorize one poem . . . "

___ c. "Each student will complete at least five of the activ-ities voluntarily . . . "

___ d. "At the end of the month each student . . . "

TURN THE PAGE

Statement *a* uses the indefinite word *several* and is *not appropriate*.

Statement *b* only specifies one behavior and is *not appropriate*. (Note: if a number was associated with "the student" the criterion would be appropriate. That is, "Half the students will memorize one poem" could be an appropriate criterion, but then you would be assessing a number of students rather than a number of activities.)

Statement *c* is correct and is *appropriate*.

Statement *d* does not specify criteria, and is *not appropriate*.

If you wish to review using "number of students" as a criterion, TURN BACK TO PAGE 71.

If you have already reviewed this topic, GO TO THE NEXT PAGE.

SUMMARY

1. The statement of *criteria* should include a *number* that you have determined to be the minimal acceptable number of students who demonstrate the approach behavior

    OR

    the minimal number of *activities* (approach behaviors) each student will demonstrate.

2. To be useful, the fulfilled criterion should indicate a trend, a pattern of approach.

3. The statement of *criteria* should be based on your knowledge of students' present behavior and upon a realistic estimate of what changes you can expect in your students.

TURN THE PAGE

Let's see how well you have learned.

Indicate which of the following are appropriate criterion statements for this situation.

Situation:

In a high school German class of above-average students the teacher wants the students to have a "desire to learn German." One approach behavior is a voluntary reading of selections from Goethe in German. Only three students in a class of twenty-five have done any outside reading thus far.

____a. Each student will read one of the five simplified excerpts from Goethe.

____b. At least ten students will read the selections from Goethe before the end of the semester.

____c. Each student will read at least half the Goethe selections.

____d. All of the students will read the excerpts in one week.

____e. Fifteen of the students will read one of the excerpts during the semester.

____f. The students will read Goethe during the semester.

____g. Three of the selections will be read by each student.

____h. Each student will leave no more than two Goethe selections unread.

GO TO THE NEXT PAGE

If you selected only *b, c, g,* and *h,* you are correct. TURN THE PAGE.

If you did not select one of these--*b, c, g,* or *h*--examine them again. Each is an appropriate statement of criteria. (Statement *h* indicates a pattern of approach as assessed by the behavior *not* demonstrated.)

Statement *a* is not based on the information about the students. "One simplified selection" is not a very difficult task for above-average German students.

Statement *d* is not realistic--it requires too much of the students in too short a time.

The results from statement *e* would not indicate a trend or pattern. One sample of behavior probably is not enough.

In statement *f* there is no indication of the number of activities or the number of students.

TURN THE PAGE

This concludes our discussion of criterion statements in affective objectives. Now you write a statement of criteria.

Situation:

A fourth-grade teacher has just begun a unit on recognizing solid geometric forms. The approach behavior she has selected is the students voluntarily bringing to class objects from home as examples of the geometric forms. Usually the majority of her thirty-five students bring things to class when they are requested to. The teacher is concerned that the students show an interest in geometry.

In the space below state appropriate criteria for assessing this attitude:

_____

_____

_____

_____

SELF-CHECK

a. Did you specify a *number* that can be calculated?

b. Did you avoid *indefinite* words?

c. Is the number specified a *number of students* or a *number of approach behaviors?*

d. Will the results indicate a trend or *pattern of approach?*

e. Are the criteria *realistic* in relation to what you were told about the students?

If you answered yes to each of these questions you are ready to write complete affective objectives. TURN TO PAGE 85.

If your answer to any of these questions was no, modify your statement on page 82 or write another statement that is appropriate for this situation. Then,

TURN TO PAGE 85

5

The Complete
Affective Objective
Putting It All Together

In the first four chapters of this booklet we have examined each part of an affective objective in some detail. Now we will put the parts together.

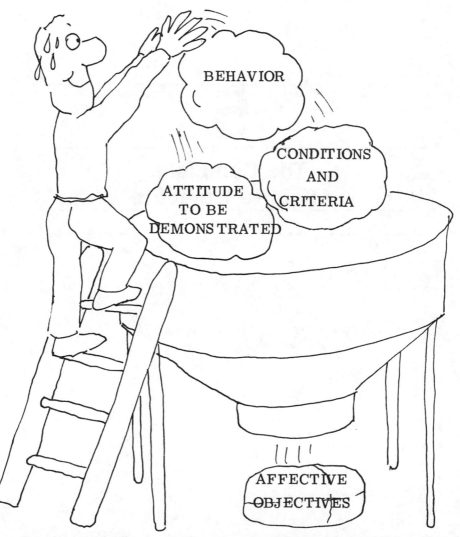

If you would like to study some examples of complete affective objectives, GO TO THE NEXT PAGE.

If you are ready to be tested, TURN TO PAGE 90.

EXAMPLE: High School Biology Class

Behavior: Coming to class early.
(High-probability, approach, directly observable)

Conditions: Teacher does not ask students to come early, but has room open so that they may; does not reward those who come early, but has biology books available for students to browse through. (Alternatives; no-cue, free-choice testing situation)

Criteria: One-third of the students will come early each day throughout the semester and 90 percent of the students will come early at least once. (Number, pattern, realistic)

Attitude: Interest in biology.

TURN THE PAGE

EXAMPLE: Sixth-Grade Social Studies

Behavior:

Asking parents questions about family life style.
(High-probability, approach, directly observable)

Conditions:

During a unit on human development the teacher discusses family life styles but does not ask individual students about their life styles. Teacher distributes a worksheet "for the students' own information" which lists questions to ask parents to help identify life styles. Teacher informs students that she will not collect the worksheets. A week later the teacher contacts one-third of the parents randomly.
(Alternatives; no-cue, free-choice testing situation)

Criteria:

At least one-half of the parents will report that their children asked them questions about their family life style.
(Number, pattern, realistic)

Attitude:

Interest in family life styles.

GO TO THE NEXT PAGE

EXAMPLE: Girls' Physical Education Class

Behavior:	Participation in extracurricular sports program. (High-probability, approach, directly observable)
Conditions:	Teacher will organize an after-school sports program involving seven sports. Program will be run by students but administered by the teacher. Program will be open to all girls. Teacher sends announcement to be read in all P. E. classes inviting all girls to participate. No school credit is given for participation. Teacher does not talk about the program during regular P. E. classes. (Alternatives; no-cue, free-choice testing situation)
Criteria:	Each girl will participate in at least one of the sports during the semester. A third of the girls will participate in at least three of the sports. (Number, pattern, realistic)
Attitude:	Desire to be physically fit.

TURN THE PAGE

What is *wrong* with this incomplete affective objective?

Junior High School Geography Class

Behavior:	Build an eight-foot globe representing the world.
Conditions:	Teacher tells class that Lincoln Junior High students have built a six-foot globe and she is sure they can do better. No grades are given for work on the globe, but the teacher promises that those who complete it will be recognized.
Criteria:	At least half the students in the class will each build a globe. The best globe will have a picture taken of it for the local newspaper.
Attitude:	Desire to learn more about geography.

Check all that apply:

___ a. No pattern of approach

___ b. Not a high-probability behavior

___ c. Not a free-choice situation

___ d. No number indicated in statement of criteria

___ e. Not realistic criteria

___ f. Not directly observable

___ g. No alternatives presented

___ h. Not a no-cue situation

___ i. Statement in wrong category

Analysis:

You should have checked *b*, *c*, *e*, *h*, and *i*.

There is a pattern of approach indicated, but a highly improbable one. The teacher has attempted to persuade the students to build the globe by promising recognition in the local newspaper. The criterion is unrealistic--a teacher could not expect one or two students to complete such a task by themselves. The students were informed about the teacher's expectations for them, so the situation was not a no-cue situation. Finally, under *criteria* a statement is included about the newspaper; this statement is really a part of the *conditions*.

Affective objectives *are* complex.

TURN THE PAGE

A comment on format:

It may be easier to write affective objectives when each part is written separately than when all parts are together in a single paragraph. Either form is acceptable. It will probably be helpful for you to write *conditions, behavior,* and *criteria* separately until you become familiar with all the characteristics of each part.

A final consideration:

Cognitive and psychomotor objectives are usually given or made available to the student so that he knows exactly what he will need to accomplish.

Do you think it would be wise to explain your affective objectives to your students in the same way?

GO TO THE NEXT PAGE

In most cases, if you told the students what you were trying to accomplish you would invalidate what you were trying to do. Remember that when students are being evaluated, the presence of an authority figure (you) tends to alter the students' responses.

In almost all cases you will *not* show your affective objectives to your students.

TURN THE PAGE

Are you ready for a quiz? Which of the following are complete affective objectives?

___ a. Each student will reveal his interest in national government by making a list of things that would happen if people stopped paying taxes. Each student who has at least five items on his list will get to read it to the class.

___ b. All students are invited to an art demonstration-lecture by a famous artist. The next day in class the teacher asks how many students have "ever heard" the famous artist speak. All art students who are really interested in art will either raise their hands or say they could not attend the presentation.

___ c. At least half of the students studying earth science will be prepared for each test during the semester. Preparation will consist of voluntary study together in student-organized study groups. Preparation will be shown by a high score on each test.

___ d. When asked to give an extemporaneous talk in senior English, one-half of the drama students will show that they enjoy speaking by volunteering.

___ e. By asking questions about furniture refinishing, at least half the shop students will show a desire to learn about furniture refinishing.

___ f. Each student will show that he wants to save money by voluntarily saving enough during the school year to buy something of his own choosing. The item purchased will be brought to school and displayed before school on the last day of class.

GO TO THE NEXT PAGE

Statements *b, d,* and *f* are complete affective objectives.

How are the students' responses influenced in statement *a* ?

What attitude is stated in statement *c* ?

What is the testing situation for statement *e* ?

Statements *a, c,* and *e* all have missing parts. Can you identify other problems? When you are satisfied that *a, c,* and *e*
are not complete affective objectives and are done studying these
statements,

TURN THE PAGE

Now it is *your* turn to write a complete affective objective. Good luck.

Remember:

Behavior: *high-probability*

                 approach

                 directly or indirectly observable

Conditions: *alternatives; no-cue, free-choice testing situation*

Criteria: *a number*

                 a pattern

                 realistic

Attitude: *interest, appreciation, or desire*

GO TO THE NEXT PAGE

For *one* of these situations write a complete affective objective in the space below.

Situation 1:

A high-school drama class meets daily. Students are fairly
attentive in class. The teacher wants students to "feel the
power of self-expression."

Situation 2:

A fifth-grade class has been studying a unit on math sets.
The teacher wants students to understand that sets are important because many real-world activities are composed of sets.

Behavior: _____

                   _____

Conditions: _____

                   _____

                   _____

                   _____

Criteria: _____

                   _____

Attitude: _____

                   _____

TURN THE PAGE

Check the pages that apply to the sections you are not sure of:

				page
Behavior:	a.	Is a student activity described?	___	8
	b.	Is the activity directly or indi-rectly observable?	___	8
	c.	Is the activity an approach be-havior?	___	16
	d.	Is the behavior high-probability?	___	24
Conditions:	e.	Is a testing situation described in which the approach behavior may occur?	___	38
	f.	Are two alternatives presented to the student?	___	39
	g.	Does the teacher influence the student's choice?	___	43
	h.	Are cues that indicate expected behavior eliminated?	___	44
	i.	If an indirect observation, are there any indications that at-titude is being evaluated?	___	48
Criteria:	j.	Is a number specified?	___	69
	k.	Would the fulfilled criteria indi-cate a pattern?	___	73

GO TO THE NEXT PAGE

page

        l.   Are the criteria realistic?   ___   71

Attitude: m. Is a descriptive statement included that indicates interest,
desire, or appreciation?   ___   2

All questions except *g* and *i* should have been answered yes.

If your objective did not meet all the criteria specified in the check list, TURN BACK TO PAGE 98 and review the pages checked before continuing.

If your objective passed this careful analysis, you have written a thorough, complete, well-thought-out affective objective.

TURN THE PAGE

CONGRATULATIONS! You should now be able to write affective objectives at both the elementary and secondary levels. The creative approaches *you* use to influence students will determine your success in developing positive student attitudes; affective objectives will help you to measure that success.

GO TO THE NEXT PAGE

6

Formulating Affective Objectives from Teaching Goals

Now What Do I Do?

Formulating Complete Affective Objectives
A Helpful Conversation

Mr. Jones--high school physics teacher who has not used affective objectives before

Mr. Smith- teacher who has used affective objectives exten-sively

Jones: I want to write some affective objectives that I can use in my teaching. How do I go about it?

Smith: Well, what goals do you have as a teacher?

Jones: My long-range goal is to have the students develop an appreciation for the complexity of the universe. More specifically, to have them become curious about why and how things work.

Smith: So you want your students to appreciate complexity and to develop their curiosity?

Jones: Yes, but more than that. I want them to develop a little self-sufficiency, so that when something goes wrong or breaks at home they won't be helpless.

Smith: Those are teaching goals that are directly related to both your teaching and the real-world activities of your students. Now can you formulate some affective ob-jectives related to these goals?

Jones: I'm not sure. I think I understand everything that is supposed to be included in a complete objective. But making one up for my own situation--that's something else.

Smith: Did you understand the examples of affective objectives in the program?

Jones: Oh yes--but the examples weren't in my subject area.

Smith: Well, the principles are the same. Let's take a spe-cific long-range teaching goal to work with. The first thing I do when writing an affective objective for my teaching is to ask myself: *"What attitude are you con-cerned about?"*

Jones: Let's work on the idea of self-sufficiency.

Smith: Fine. When I have the attitude clearly in mind I ask: *"What will you accept as evidence of this attitude?"*

Jones: What do you mean?

Smith: Well, do you recall what approach behaviors are?

Jones: Those are behaviors that you can observe which tell you that a student is or wants to be associated with a topic.

Smith: And from a pattern of these behaviors you should be willing to infer or to assume that a certain attitude is present. But we must be careful in the assumptions we make. Our inferences will be reliable only if they are based on a good deal of knowledge--knowledge about many approach behaviors or knowledge about the cir-cumstances in which the behavior occurred.

Jones: I see.

Smith: What behaviors will you accept as evidence of self-sufficiency?

Jones: I know John Billings has this--he is always fixing tele-visions, radios, and old cars. I don't think he has had any courses in electronics, either.

Smith: Do many other students do this sort of thing?

Jones: No, but I wouldn't expect them to. John has exceptional mechanical aptitude.

Smith: So his behavior is not what you would call high-probability?

Jones: No. But I wish more of my students were like that. At least so that when something mechanical did go wrong they would try to apply their knowledge.

Smith: Could you formulate an objective with that as the approach behavior?

Jones: You mean have the students fix something to show that they are somewhat self-sufficient?

Smith: Would you accept that as evidence of their attitude?

Jones: Yes, that would be one evidence. But how am I going to know when they fix something? I can't follow them around outside of class.

Smith: The purpose of a testing situation in an affective objective is to provide a setting in which students can perform the approach behavior. *Under what circumstances must these behaviors occur for your inferences to be valid and useful to you?*

Jones: I see. I could set up some sort of situation, without telling the students, to see how many of them would voluntarily fix something in class that was broken.

Smith: You have the idea.

Jones: Should I plan to do this at a certain time during the year?

Smith: Because this is a long-range goal, I would not relate it to any particular unit or topic. In fact, I would probably set up a number of situations like this during the year, so that I could give the students a chance to show a pattern of approach. *Now, how will you know when or if the objective has been achieved? (What criteria will you use to judge completion or success?)*

Jones: How *do* I determine criteria for something like this?
          I've never done it before.

Smith: This is always a problem when you begin assessing
          attitude. For a long-range goal you really need some
          information from which you can make comparisons.
          You need to know how many students will exhibit this
          behavior *before* you attempt to influence them.

Jones: That's why you suggested doing this a number of times
          during the year?

Smith: Yes. That way you can tell if your influence has
          changed their behavior over a long period of time.

Jones: But I thought you weren't supposed to try to influence
          the student's behavior.

Smith: You are not supposed to try to influence student be-
          havior in the testing situation. The rest of the time
          you will probably be doing all you can to influence
          their behavior. And it is their behavior that indicates
          their attitude, remember.

Jones: What does my objective look like now?

Smith: You've specified the attitude, the approach behavior,
          and the general plan for a testing situation, and you
          have an idea how to establish criteria to evaluate
          change.

Jones: Sounds great. Do I follow this same procedure to
          develop affective objectives for short-range goals?

Smith: Yes. First,   determine the attitude to be evaluated.
                Second, determine what student behavior you
                         will accept as evidence of the attitude.
                Third,   determine the circumstances under
                         which the behavior can occur.
                Fourth, determine criteria that will show you
                         a pattern of approach.

Of course, for each of these steps there are other considerations which were explained in the program.

Jones: This has been very helpful. I have always been concerned about the attitudes my students had. This should help me evaluate those attitudes more accurately than I have before.

Smith: Good luck.

APPENDIX

Using Avoidance Behaviors as Indicators of Attitude

Attitude is shown as much by what we avoid as by what we approach. However, an avoidance response is often not of the same duration as an approach response. That is, if a person approaches a topic, he will usually maintain contact with the topic over a period of time. At any point an observer may see him associated with the topic.

Avoidance behaviors, on the other hand, occur usually as an attempt is made to bring a person into contact with a topic. Unless an observer was aware of this moment, he would not be able to discern a person's moving away from the topic. If a person is involved in one activity, he is at the same time *not* involved in a great many other activities. We cannot justly say that he is avoiding all these other activities. He may be neutral or he might approach them if he had an opportunity.

It therefore becomes quite difficult to specify avoidance be-haviors as a part of an affective objective. Unless the testing situation is tightly controlled, you cannot safely infer that a person has turned away from or avoided a topic.

Avoidance behaviors are generally actions in which a person chooses to *not do* or *not be involved or associated with* some-thing. If the student response you want consists of "avoiding something," then you may be able to use avoidance behaviors in your affective objectives. For example:

Topic: U. S. government

Attitude: Desire to preserve the democratic system.

Desired avoidance behaviors, from which you might infer the at-titude:

   General Behaviors:

      1.   Not joining student riots

2. Not supporting revolutionary groups

3. Not supporting anti-American causes

Specific Behaviors:

1. Student does not come to an after-school lecture on "why we need revolution in America today."

2. Student leaves room when speaker speaks against the democratic system.

3. Student argues against changing the democratic system.

You may not agree with the behaviors listed.

When a student is arguing against something, is he showing avoidance for the thing argued against, or approach for the thing he is inherently supporting? Note that for this attitude a number of *approach behaviors* could also be specified:

1. Voting when elections are held

2. Contributing money to a political party

3. Canvassing the neighborhood to gain support for a local candidate.

Some paradoxes are created when an avoidance behavior is the desired student response. A health teacher presenting a lesson on the hazards of smoking might want her students to *approach* (be associated with) the topic so that they could learn the hazards of smoking. Subsequently she would want her students to *avoid* (the act of) smoking. Her concern is twofold: to develop a positive attitude toward "learning about the hazards of smoking" and to develop a negative attitude toward "acquiring the habit of smoking."

The same general problem exists when you attempt to develop objectives for such personal characteristics as trustworthiness, neatness, punctuality, honesty, responsibility, etc. A person could give evidence that he was "neat" by:

    1. Wearing a lint-free suit.

    2. Keeping an office well organized.

OR BY

    1. Not wearing a suit that has lint on it.

    2. Not cluttering an office.

The solution? Usually when you think an avoidance response is the desired student behavior you can also identify approach behaviors that are somewhat parallel.

(As you work with affective objectives you will undoubtedly develop procedures that work well for you. The authors are still collecting information in this important area of education and would gladly welcome inquiries and/or suggestions.)